Newsmakers™

Kim Jong Il

Leader of North Korea

Joyce Hart

ROSEN
PUBLISHING®

New York

Published in 2008 by The Rosen Publishing Group, Inc.
29 East 21st Street, New York, NY 10010

Library of Congress Cataloging-in-Publication Data

Hart, Joyce, 1954–
Kim Jong Il: leader of North Korea / Joyce Hart.—1st ed.
    p. cm.—(Newsmakers)
Includes bibliographical references and index.
ISBN-13: 978-1-4042-1901-4
ISBN-10: 1-4042-1901-3
1. Jong, il Kim, 1942—Juvenile literature. 2. Heads of state—Korea
(North)—Biography—Juvenile literature. 3. Korea (North)—Politics
and government—Juvenile literature. 4. Il Sung, Kim, 1912–1994—
Juvenile literature.
I. Title.
DS934.6.K44H37 2008
951.9304'3092—dc22

[B]
                                                          2006101216

Manufactured in the United States of America

On the cover: Foreground: Kim Jong Il salutes troops during a
military parade. Background: North Korean soldiers march during a
ceremony honoring the fifty-fifth anniversary of the nation's
Communist government.

CONTENTS

INTRODUCTION

K im Jong Il is a mysterious head of state, a dictator who rules North Korea from behind a curtain of secrecy. Visiting reporters are seldom allowed to ask questions. Most information is speculation from diplomats, who are rarely given a chance of meeting directly with him. Satellites that spy on Kim's and North Korea's activities from outer space and defectors who were once close to Kim give some clues about the inscrutable leader. Most of the concrete information on the dictator comes in

Kim Jong Il salutes his troops during a military parade celebrating North Korea's fifty-fifth anniversary.

the form of propaganda that he publishes and distributes around the world.

In October 2006, Kim shocked everyone when he sent the loudest message yet in the twelve years of his leadership, a message that was heard around the globe. He detonated a nuclear bomb in an underground test, proving to his neighbors and political enemies that North Korea possesses the most powerful form of weaponry. Since Kim first took over leadership of North Korea, he had denied accusations that he was building up the country's military program, but his actions in 2006 proved that he had been lying.

Many countries were caught off guard by North Korea's weapons development, which had progressed so far that Kim could send a bomb not only to the surrounding countries of Japan, South Korea, Russia, or China, but also to the shores of the United States. Because of North Korea's advanced weapons, the world had to face the fear of a potentially devastating threat: nuclear war.

Since Kim Jong Il first took power in 1994, he has been moving steadily in a direction that makes other world leaders increasingly nervous. One of North Korea's most dominant political beliefs is that it must have a strong army to protect itself from being overtaken by a more powerful country. To this end, Kim has overseen the development of an army estimated to consist of 1.2 million soldiers, the fourth-largest army in the world. Suspicions of Kim's nuclear weapons program began in 2003, when the leader pulled out of a Cold War–era nuclear disarmament treaty and restarted the process of extracting weapons-grade plutonium. Shortly afterward, rumors began to spread that North Korea was developing a nuclear bomb. Just a few months prior to the October 2006 test, Kim launched seven missiles. Each missile landed harmlessly in the Sea of Japan without physical damages to any person or object. However, the missiles marked the beginning of the injured relationships the leader would have with the rest of the world.

Unlike his predecessor, his father, who was outgoing and charismatic, Kim Jong II is rarely seen or heard. People who have known him say that he is insecure in public, constantly on the vigil for potential assassinators and unable to trust anyone, even his own soldiers.

Not only is Kim one of the world's most dangerous leaders, but he is also one of the most desperate for financial aid and political power. Despite North Korea's disintegrating economy and the starvation of millions of his people, Kim spends almost one-third of North Korea's budget on military expenditures. He has put a lot of that money into the expansion of North Korea's long-range missiles program as well as his country's capabilities to create biological and chemical weapons.

Leaders from countries such as South Korea, Russia, China, Japan, and the United States have no idea how far Kim Jong Il will go or what he plans to do with his weapons. His plans could drastically affect the welfare of these countries, as well as the rest of the world. Diplomats, politicians, and military specialists from around the world watch, from a distance, and wait to see signals from Kim, trying to guess the dictator's next step.

CHAPTER ONE

A LIFE SHROUDED IN MYTH

Official accounts say that the day of Kim Jong Il's birth, in the early 1940s, was marked with omens: a message delivered by a sparrow; a double rainbow; and at night, an unusually bright star. The exact details and truths of his life, however, are few. What is known is that Kim faced many challenges in his youth. He was born, literally, in the middle of a war; he was motherless for half of his childhood; and as an adult, he could never step out of the shadow of his father, North Korea's first-ever leader.

Other events that might have caused difficulty, although it is impossible to know if Kim Jong Il thought of them as challenges, were the myths that were built around him and his father. Whether Kim knew the difference between things that actually happened in his life and the mythical stories is not known. What is known is that there are many inconsistencies between historically recorded events and the so-called approved biographies of himself. It is also known that Kim has lived a very isolated and secretive life, possibly due to the disparity between the facts of his life and its fiction. The mythology that surrounds Kim's beginnings may be due to his grip on the information that he authorizes to be released about himself and his rule.

Several official biographies say Kim was born on North Korea's highest and most sacred peak, Mount Paektu, on February 16, 1942. Biographies claim that the sounds of guns were the Kim children's lullabies, as both of Kim Jong Il's parents were soldiers in the military. Kim Jong Il was the first child in the family, but he had a number of siblings, many of whom were half-siblings. Like other details of Kim's life, how many siblings he had and the identities of their mothers are unclear.

Kim's actual birth date may have been changed in official accounts because in 1942 his father would have been the auspicious age of thirty when his son was born, further mythicizing the birth of North Korea's future leader. Conflicting with the authorized accounts, historic records in the Soviet Union say that Kim was born in Siberia in 1941. At that time, Kim Il Sung, Kim Jong Il's father, was a captain in the Soviet army and was stationed there. Kim's birth was recorded under the Russian form of his name, Yuri Irsenovich Kim.

Kim lived in Siberia until the end of the Second World War in 1945. After the war, Kim Jong Il and his mother, Kim Jong-suk, returned to North Korea in a Soviet ship, landing at Songbong. His father was waiting for them at a large Japanese-style home in Pyongyang. Pyongyang what would eventually become the capital of North Korea.

Two major tragedies struck the Kim family during Jong Il's childhood: When Jong Il was six, his three-year-old brother, Shura Kim, died in a drowning accident. In 1949, Jong-suk died from complications of childbirth, leaving the eight-year-old Jong Il without a mother.

Kim Il Sung, known for his charismatic public demeanor, talks with college students in Pyongyang in 1957.

A SPOILED AND LONELY CHILDHOOD

Kim Jong Il's childhood was a lonely one. His father was a notorious womanizer who always had affairs with women even while married, according to Bradley K. Martin, author of the book *Under the Loving Care of the Fatherly Leader*.

Between the state affairs and sexual affairs, Kim Il Sung was seldom home. During the Korean War (1950–1953), Jong Il, motherless and with an absentee father, moved with some of his relatives to the more isolated northernmost parts of Korea to get away from the hazards of war. Later, the family moved to China, while his father stayed in Korea to fight in the war.

Kim Il Sung later remarried a woman named Kim Song-ae. Kim Il Sung and his second wife eventually had a son. Song-ae tried her best to diminish Jong Il in his father's eyes and promote her own son. This reportedly caused psychological hardships for the young Jong Il.

Jong Il did find attention from Korean officials, who doted on the boy, believing from the start that he would eventually become the designated heir of their country. These people, according to Under the Loving Care of the Fatherly Leader, "deferred to the eldest son of the country's top leader as if he were a little prince, thus encouraging the bully in him." In other words, the young boy was spoiled, and by the time he graduated from college, Kim Jong Il had gained the reputation of being "wild, recklessly impulsive and, by turns, cruel and warm-hearted, even extravagantly generous."

EDUCATION

When Kim Jong Il was a teenager, he enrolled at the Namsan School in Pyongyang, a school where only the children of officials approved by Kim Il Sung could attend. Accounts have been made that people whose children were not eligible to attend this elitist school nicknamed it a "school for nobility," which was ironic for a nation that was allegedly built upon Communist theories that denied a system of social classes.

Although Jong Il had traveled with his father to Moscow prior to entering college, which spread rumors and speculations that Jong Il might receive his advanced education abroad, in 1960 he entered the Kim Il Sung University in Pyongyang. This university was the most prestigious and comprehensive school of higher education in North Korea. Because Kim Il Sung's political ideals were, in many areas, at odds with the Communist philosophies of both the Soviet Union and China, it was believed that he had decided not to send his son abroad for his education. He wanted his son to gain his political education in North Korea so that Jong Il would understand North Korea's specific brand of Communism.

Kim Il Sung University

Kim Il Sung University was founded in 1946 as the first university in North Korea. Today, its campus is made up of relatively modern high-rise buildings. The student population is rather small, only about 12,000, which is covered by a faculty of 6,000 teachers. It is a tough school to get into, and only about one in every five students who apply is accepted. The university contains two major departments: social science and natural science, the latter of which includes branches focused on physics and atomic energy.

While in college, Jong Il, according to the book *Great Leader, Kim Jong Il*, "with his wide knowledge and natural frankness . . . was good at everything." Not only did he excel in his studies, but he also participated in and led youth political groups. It was the role of college students, Kim Jong Il would later say, to gain a revolutionary outlook of the world.

While at Kim Il Sung University, Kim Jong Il majored in political economy, a field that would become an increasingly popular choice for students. While Kim was still an undergraduate, he reportedly took an active part in revising the textbooks from which the university professors taught their subjects. He told his teachers that they did not fully comprehend his father's philosophy of economics and suggested they incorporate his ideology into their teachings.

Kim Il Sung *(seated)* with his son, Kim Jong Il, at a 1980 Korean Workers' Party convention.

Kim did not limit his criticism to the field of economics. He also suggested changes in the textbooks of politics, philosophy, history, and science. All these studies were to reflect the principles of his father, Kim Jong Il suggested, regardless of the fact that Kim Il Sung was a man who had led a revolution but had not graduated from high school.

Kim Jong Il often brought armloads of his father's books to his fellow students and reportedly organized a movement of students whom he challenged to read, according to *Under the Loving Care of the Fatherly Leader*, "ten thousand pages a year from books by and about Kim Il Sung." These books were to be read over and over again until the students fully grasped his father's ideas.

As a student, Kim was reportedly a prolific writer. By some accounts, during his four years in college, he wrote more than 1,000 papers, mostly espousing his father's ideology. A few days before graduating in 1963, Kim supposedly delivered one of his best pieces of writing about socialism. However, his works were not made public until twenty-one years after he graduated, when he was being tailored to become his father's heir. This has raised doubts whether Kim Jong Il is the legitimate author of the works attributed to him, or if the papers had been written or heavily edited by someone else.

Kim Jong Il did not spend all his time at university studying, however. Some accounts depict him as a playboy who loved fast cars, pretty women, and lots of fattening food. It was during his time at Kim Il Sung University that Kim Jong Il took on the pudgy weight that would characterize his later image, one that stands in clear opposition to most other lean Korean youths of his time.

CHAPTER TWO

KOREA'S HISTORY OF WAR AND COLONIZATION

K im Jong Il's birth occurred in the midst of a great political process that was unfolding in North Korea. Kim Il Sung, as the first leader of the newly formed country, created the path that his son would eventually follow. But the path that Kim Il Sung took to leadership was a long one. Kim Jong Il's father was involved in, and was often the instigator of, many critical developments. During Kim Il Sung's lifetime, Korea was a colony that had experienced two wars as well as domestic uprisings. By the time of Kim Il Sung's reign in 1948, Korea was no longer unified, but had become two countries whose political divisions were deep.

Throughout most of its modern history, Korea has been used as a stepping stone. With the powerful countries of China and the Soviet Union (now Russia and other countries) to the north, and Japan to the east of the peninsula,

Koreans have had to ally themselves with one or another of these countries—or else become completely dominated. Korea has been looked upon as a source of cheap labor and farming land, and has been eyed for its natural resources. Numerous wars have been fought as governments have tried to take ownership of the tiny 85,000-square-mile (220,149 square kilometers) peninsula. Millions of Koreans have been killed. Those remaining have gone through political transitions that at one point threatened to annihilate the Korean language and culture.

Today, the country is divided into two political halves, with a demilitarized zone separating the north from the south, similar, in theory, to the Berlin Wall in Germany that divided the country east and west. Democratic influences helped to carve the future for the south, and Communist powers helped to form the north. Koreans who had together endured centuries of hardships have been divided by their governments for the last fifty or so years.

PRE-NINETEENTH-CENTURY KOREA

Relationships between the people of the Korean peninsula and their neighbors have gone through various periods of war followed by peaceful coexistence. In its earlier history, Korea was heavily influenced by China, and the two countries were once tied together, in the late fourteenth century, in their efforts to fight the Mongols who had invaded both China and Korea. Beginning in the sixteenth century, Korea suffered invasions from Japan, followed by successive invasions by China. For short periods of time, Japan controlled large portions of Korea, but that country was never able to dominate the entire peninsula until centuries later.

NINETEENTH-CENTURY KOREA

In the nineteenth century, Western countries (Britain, France, Russia, and the United States, to name a few) saw Korea as an excellent dumping ground for their goods. They tried to set up trade in Korea and interfered in Korea's politics in the process. They wanted to force their merchandise on Korea, but Korea refused. Koreans did not want to become capitalist like the Western countries. Capitalism conflicted with their Confucian beliefs, which they had adopted from China. In general, Confucian teachings stress the family over the individual, loyalty to the state, and honesty and benevolence toward others. In contrast, capitalism's main goal is to make a profit, sometimes at a cost to other people and the environment, and the emphasis is on the individual, not the family or the state.

Korea tried to protect itself from being forced into trade negotiations by closing its borders to all other countries except China. This did not stop Japan, which, beginning in the 1870s, threatened Korea with war if it did not sign trade treaties. Japan had a military that significantly outpowered Korean forces. Japan had limited resources and craved the fertile Korean land, especially in the south, where it could grow rice and soybeans. It also wanted to

tap into Korea's sources of coal and iron ore, resources that were in desperate need in Japan as it entered the industrial age.

In 1876, Korea was coerced into signing what would be called the Treaty of Ganghwa with Japan. Some Korean officials believed that this would create an amiable relationship between the two countries, which would lead to Korea learning the technologies that the Japanese had mastered and were using to modernize their country. Unfortunately, the treaty did not turn out as the officials had planned. Japan took advantage of the agreement, draining resources from Korea and making exorbitant profits back home and running many Korean merchants out of business. Trade was not the only thing that interested the Japanese. They also wanted to make Korea independent from China. This would help pave

This map shows the division of the Korean peninsula.

the way for Japan to annex Korea, its close neighbor to the west.

Not everyone in Korea was pleased with the strong connection with Japan. More conservative Koreans remained loyal to China. In 1884, there was a clash between pro-Japan and pro-China groups in Korea, a civil conflict that would lead Japanese and Chinese armies into the First Sino-Japanese War (1894–1895). In the end, the more modernized Japanese military won a relatively easy victory. After the war, Japan's influence over Korea continued to escalate, specifically in the south. However, there was another force to the northwest that Japan would eventually have to contend with: the Soviet Union.

EARLY TWENTIETH-CENTURY KOREA

Russia had been expanding its influence on the northern part of the Korean peninsula. On the last day of the year in 1903, the Japanese government gave Russia an ultimatum. It demanded that either Russia move its troops

U.S. president Theodore Roosevelt helped Russia and Japan broker a peace agreement concerning their claims to the Korean peninsula during the Russo-Japanese War (1904–1905).

out of Korea so Japan could take over the entire peninsula, or face battle. Two months later, the two countries were in the heat of the Russo-Japanese War (1904–1905). Japan delivered a significant blow to the Russian military, the first time an Asian force had succeeded in doing so to a Western country. With Japan running out of money and unrest at home for the Russian military, both sides were ready to listen to U.S. president Theodore Roosevelt (1858–1919), who helped the two countries broker a peace agreement. In the process, Japanese control of Korea was recognized, and Russia pulled back its hold on the northern part of the peninsula. In 1907, Japan made Korea a protectorate state. Three years later, Japan annexed Korea. The consequences of Japan's imperialism in Korea included heavy taxation, slavery-like forced labor, and destruction of Korea's political system. A steady and heavy depletion of Korea's resources followed.

CHAPTER THREE

NORTH KOREA'S FIRST LEADER: THE TIME OF KIM IL SUNG

By 1919, the Korean people had had enough of the nearly ten years of oppressive Japanese rule. Thirty-three Korean protesters created a declaration of independence and read it aloud in front of a huge gathering in Seoul. The news of this reading spread fast throughout the restive country, mobilizing Koreans up and down the peninsula to organize pro-liberation demonstrations in what would eventually be known as the March First Movement. Japanese officials stepped in to control the uprising, and 7,000 Koreans died in the demonstrations.

Even though the protesters did not get the independence that they had sought, the demonstrations helped advance Korea toward independence. Freedom-fighting Koreans set up a provisional government, meant to spearhead a liberation effort, in Shanghai, China. Although many of the restrictions on Koreans by the Japanese remained in effect, including forced labor, the Japanese made small concessions after the uprising. These changes were referred to as a new cultural policy and included a slight leniency in the Japanese-controlled press and a substitution from a military to a civilian police force. These changes did not last long, however. All were reversed when Japan went to war with China over the Korean peninsula.

KIM IL SUNG'S EARLY YEARS

Kim Jong Il's father, Kim Il Sung, was born during a time when Korea was at the brink of great change, in 1912, outside the city of Pyongyang in the northern part of the country. In the years following the massive March First protests, many Koreans fled to China and a region of China called Manchuria, an area that links northwestern Korea to northeastern China. Kim Il Sung's father had been imprisoned during the 1919 protests, and so he moved his family to Manchuria, where he thought they'd be safer.

NORTH KOREA'S FIRST LEADER:
THE TIME OF KIM IL SUNG

Kim Il Sung at the beginning of his role as leader of
North Korea in 1953.

Perhaps due to his political upbringing, Kim Il
Sung showed leadership qualities and an interest
in politics at a young age. While in Manchuria, at
the age of fourteen, Kim Il Sung organized a
study group, which he called the Down with
Imperialism Union, a group that was influenced
by the theories of Communism. Russia, by then,
was part of the Union of Soviet Socialist

Republics (USSR) and was controlled by a
Communist government. The movement was
slowly taking over China. Among the theories
that the youths found appealing was Communism's
proclamation that the government, not rich
capitalists, should control the country. In 1925,
Korean exiles in Manchuria formed their own
branch of a Communist party, which Kim Il
Sung joined two years later. In 1927, Kim Il Sung
was expelled from school for his political
beliefs. By 1929, at seventeen years old, he
found himself as a political prisoner. Although
the southern portions of China were being
swept into a Communist movement, the
northern portions of the country, where Il Sung
lived, were strictly against the movement. This
was soon to change.

A Reputable Fighter

In 1931, the Japanese invaded Manchuria. Now
the Chinese and the exiled Koreans had a
mutual enemy. Groups of guerrilla soldiers, both
Chinese and Koreans, worked together, targeting

outposts of Japanese soldiers in northern Korea. Kim Il Sung was one of the leaders of those raids. Kim's military training intensified when the Japanese drove the Korean guerrilla forces out of Manchuria, and he decided to join the Soviet Union forces in Siberia. Kim's reputation as a fighter was known all throughout Korea. In fact, Japan, at one time, had gone so far as to promise a sizeable amount of money for Kim Il Sung's capture.

WORLD WAR II

By the late 1930s, Japan was on the brink of entering World War II as part of the Axis powers, which mainly included Italy and Germany against the Allies, primarily comprising the Soviet Union, England, and the United States. On the home front, uprisings continued throughout Korea as Japanese rule tightened on the peninsula. Korean language and history were forbidden in schools, with all Korean textbooks replaced by those written by the Japanese. Attendance at Japanese Shinto shrines became mandatory. By the beginning of World War II, Japan was well on its way to exterminating all Korean culture, even to the point of commanding that every Korean person change his or her name to a Japanese one. To fight against this repression, Koreans fled to Manchuria and created their own armies, such as the Korean Liberation Army, the People's Liberation Army, and the National Revolution Army. Some of these units fought with the Allied forces during World War II. Meanwhile, other Koreans were forced to fight with the Japanese military.

THE THIRTY-EIGHTH PARALLEL

World War II ended in 1945. Germany surrendered to the Allied forces, and members of the Soviet army swept through Manchuria and into Korea. Japan's defeat came in 1945 after the United States dropped two nuclear bombs on the country—first in Hiroshima, then three days later, in Nagasaki. The United States and the Soviet Union split occupation of Korea at the thirty-eighth parallel. The United States took control of the southern portion and the Soviet

UN trucks cross the border between North and South Korea during the Korean War (1950–1953).

Union took the northern half, marking the first political division of Korea.

That same year, the government of the Soviet Union made Kim Il Sung the leader of the Provisional People's Party. He moved his country firmly in his control by nationalizing almost every industry and, therefore, placing the economy under government control. As leader of the Korean Workers' Party (KWP), a conglomeration of many Communist parties from both the north and south of Korea, Il Sung eliminated all dissenters through execution or imprisonment. Over the next five years, North Korea's leader organized a large army, equipped and trained by the Soviet military under the approval of Joseph Stalin (1879–1953), leader of the Soviet Union from 1928 until 1953. When it was Kim Il Sung's turn to form a new country, he used Stalin's government as a model.

Meanwhile, in the southern part of the peninsula, the United States, along with the United Nations, set up elections that were to be held only in the south. The freedom-fighting Koreans in the north and the south tried to stop the elections, since this would make the split between the two parts of the nation that much more indelible. The elections were held, however, and Syngman Rhee, a man who was considered merely a puppet of the U.S. government, was elected the first president of South Korea in 1948. Rhee, who despised the concepts of Communism, represented the opposite political philosophy of Kim Il Sung, further distancing

South Korea from the north. Rhee was not a popular leader, and his election would later be contested. He would eventually be pushed out of office and would die in exile in Hawaii.

Syngman Rhee

Syngman Rhee (1875–1965) was the first elected president of South Korea. Rhee was a right-wing conservative who wanted nothing to do with Communism. He was educated in the United States. After World War II, Rhee returned to Korea. He found support from the U.S. government and ran for the position of first president of the newly democratized Republic of Korea (South Korea).

Rhee was elected to office in 1948, but once in power, he increasingly drifted away from a democratic platform and became more autocratic. Many dissidents to his rule were mysteriously silenced, with rising suspicion that Rhee had ordered their murders. Despite this, he maintained the presidency through the Korean War, possibly by rigging elections. Protests grew more numerous and intense until Rhee was thrown out of power in April 1960. He retreated to Hawaii, where he eventually died.

U.S. general Douglas MacArthur speaks with the first South Korean president, Syngman Rhee, in 1948.

The Communists of North Korea were disappointed by events in the south. However, the northern portion of the country had to be unified, so in 1948, the Soviets appointed the war hero Kim Il Sung as the prime minister of the newly established Democratic People's Republic of Korea, the official name of the north. The southern portion of the peninsula was referred to as the Republic of Korea. One year later, in 1949, Kim Il Sung was also made the chairman of the KWP. In that same year, both the United States and the Soviet Union withdrew most of their forces from the Korean peninsula, marking the first time since the turn of the century that Koreans ruled Koreans.

KOREAN WAR

Both Rhee and Kim orchestrated small battles in 1949, trying to assert their strength to reunite the country under their own rule. Rhee wanted to encourage unification under a right-wing, capitalist democracy. Kim, meanwhile, promoted Communism. In 1950, having built up a strong military force financially supported by the Soviets, Kim was ready for an outright invasion of the south. Stalin reportedly did not initially approve of Kim's desires to invade the south.

Kim began to move his forces on June 25, 1950. Seoul was captured three days later. The south was no match for the North Koreans, or at least that is what Kim had hoped. Kim also thought the people in the south would support him and quickly surrender. He had not planned, however, on fighting a war against the United States.

When U.S. president Harry Truman learned of Kim's invasion, he feared the beginning of another world war. Troops were sent in as quickly as possible, but not quickly enough. Kim and his forces pushed past Seoul and pressed South Korean and U.S. forces into a small southeast corner of the peninsula. U.S. reinforcements, in the form of the U.S. Air Force, and UN troops finally arrived and began pushing Kim and his armies north. Officials in China and the Soviet Union became concerned that if the U.S. forces reached the northern borders of Korea, they might not stop. China then sent troops to help Kim. The war progressed through a series of back-and-forth invasions until 1953, when the sides confronted each other at the thirty-eighth parallel, the division line that had originally been set up by the United States and the Soviet Union. On July 27, newly elected U.S. president Dwight D. Eisenhower, under a proposal created by a UN delegation, declared a cease-fire. To this day, the Demilitarized Zone (DMZ) exists along the thirty-eighth parallel, with South Korean troops on one side and North Korean troops on the other. No peace agreement has ever been signed by either side. By the end of the Korean War, it was estimated that about 150,000 U.S. and UN soldiers and civilians, more than a million Chinese, and nearly four million Koreans had been killed.

CREATING A POLITICAL IDEOLOGY

After the Korean War, Kim Sung Il traveled to Moscow and Beijing to request money to rebuild his country. In the process of acquiring the Soviet Union's and China's assistance to reestablish North Korea's economy, Kim developed a political philosophy that was all his own. He took part of his ideas from Stalin and created his own interpretation of Marxism. Another influence came from Chinese dictator Mao Tse-tung's (1893–1976) political ideology. However, the foundation of Kim's ideas was grounded in an ancient principle upon which Koreans had built their country. Based on Confucianism, the principle was called *juche* (pronounced ju-chay), which translates as "self reliance." Kim conformed the ancient philosophy to meet his and his country's needs in the twentieth century.

Chinese leader Mao Tse-tung (1893–1976) and Russian leader Joseph Stalin (1879–1953) greatly influenced Kim Il Sung's political philosophy for a Communist state.

The main idea behind juche (sometimes referred to as Kim-Il-Sungism by Kim Jong Il) is that a country should be allowed to develop without becoming a puppet government of other, more powerful political entities. To accomplish this, citizens are to band together, practicing self-sacrifice if necessary, in order to build the state. The people are the masters of their destinies but must work as one unit and defer all power and allegiance to the leader. Kim Il Sung was able to accomplish two things by creating and focusing on a new ideology. First, he would lead his people away from the philosophical influence of China and the Soviet Union and, thus, differentiate North Korea as an independent nation. Second, it would establish the groundwork for Kim to become the supreme dictator in his land. There are three major components of juche: chagu, charip, and chawi. Under the principle of chagu, which calls for domestic and foreign independence, Kim held that all nations should be considered equal, with intervention by a more powerful country on a weaker one strictly forbidden. Yielding to a foreign power is also unacceptable. Instead of powerful domination, juche calls for cooperation, especially among peers, which for North Korea meant the Soviet Union, China, Cuba, and other socialist or Communist governments.

The principle of charip, which means economic independence, requires the country to strive for complete economic self-sufficiency. The idea is that without an independent economy, there can be no domestic and foreign independence.

Fearing invasion from countries Kim referred to as imperialists, the third main principle of his ideology, chawi, establishes military independence. This translates into a North Korean policy of a strong military to be able to protect the country's political and economic independence.

Joseph Stalin

Joseph Stalin was the leader of the Soviet Union from 1928 until his death in 1953. He was a member of the Bolshevik Party, founded by Vladimir Lenin (1870–1924), who followed the philosophy developed by Karl Marx (1818–1883). The Bolsheviks eventually became the Communist Party of the Soviet Union. Following his interpretations of Communism, Stalin forced farmers to provide food for industrial workers, which led to thousands of peasants not having enough food for themselves and starving to death. Also under his rule, thousands were called traitors and were either shot or sent to prison camps, where they died. These and other practices of Stalin's were later adopted by Kim Il Sung in his rise in power in North Korea.

PUTTING JUCHE TO WORK

Around 1957, Kim Il Sung created and promoted
various plans to inspire North Koreans to
work hard and fast, and to practice self-sacrifice
for the good of their country. Under these
plans, he poured effort into production of
heavy metals and fuels, modern equipment for
agricultural production, and military weapons.
Extensive aid from China and the Soviet Union
helped North Korea accomplish Kim's goals.
At the expense of North Korea's productivity,
workers suffered, toiling for long hours and
receiving poor wages.

Theoretically, Kim Il Sung's political ideology
would lead North Koreans to self-sufficiency,
depending on no one but themselves. In the
beginning, as the ideology was put to work, it
looked as if it might be successful: North
Korea's economy was strong, even stronger
than the U.S.-supported South Korean economy.
That would change significantly by the time
Kim Jong Il took over his father's role.

CHAPTER FOUR

THE RISE OF KIM JONG IL

By the time Kim Jong Il graduated from Kim Il Sung University in 1963, he began taking steps toward ruling the country founded by his father. Immediately upon graduation from college, he began working his way into his father's government by becoming involved in the system of the KWP. He first went to work as the director of the KWP's prestigious Central Committee's Organizational Bureau, what has been referred to as the nerve center of his father's regime. Kim Jong Il's position instigated speculation that his father was considering Jong Il as his heir long before Kim Il Sung made his choice public. In 1966, Jong Il was named supervising director, and a year later, he became the section leader of the KWP Central Committee's Arts and Culture Bureau.

In his position at the Arts and Culture Bureau, Kim Jong Il found a home. He had long been attracted to movies and took the position

Shin Sang-ok, a famous South Korean movie director, was supposedly kidnapped by Kim Jong Il and forced to make movies for the North Korean leader in the 1980s.

to heart. It was during this time that he wrote his revolutionary opera *Sea of Blood*, which focused on exaggerated heroism during the war against Japan in the 1930s. The opera drew great applause from his fellow citizens and continues to be shown in North Korean theaters to this day, having been staged more than 1,500 times, by one account. *Sea of Blood* was later adapted as a film, and, according to people who have visited Pyongyang, it is the only movie in town.

In 1970, Kim gained his most influential position, up to that time, as the assistant chief of the committee's Propaganda and Agitation Bureau. Three years later, in 1973, he was the chief. It was during these years that Kim Jong Il helped to raise the status of his father's image in the eyes of the North Korean people. He promoted the personality cult that eventually would claim that Kim Il Sung was a god. In 1972, Kim Jong Il oversaw the erection of a giant gold statue of his father. He also began the ritual of required bowing to statues of Kim Il Sung. It also became mandatory for every house in North Korea to display an image of Kim Il Sung.

Kim Jong Il was not the only member of the Kim family who served in the Central Committee

Kim Jong Il and the Movies

To make his movie *Sea of Blood*, Kim Jong Il reportedly kidnapped a South Korean movie director and his actress wife. The story, as reported in London's *Guardian* newspaper, involves Shin Sang-ok, a director of "legendary stature" and his wife, Choi Eun-hee, who were kidnapped, brought to North Korea, and imprisoned for four years. They were reportedly forced by Kim to make his movie and to be held captive in North Korea. Shin went on to make seven other movies for Kim before he and his wife made a dramatic escape in 1986 while they were on business in Austria.

of the KWP. Kim Il Sung's second wife, Kim Song-ae, was a member. So was one of his daughters, his son-in-law, his cousin, and a brother-in-law. Kim Il Sung's younger brother Kim Yong-ju was for a time considered the favorite to succeed Kim Il Sung and, like Kim Jong Il, was climbing the ladder in the Central Committee of the KWP. However, in 1975, Kim Yong-ju mysteriously disappeared from the public. He would reappear in the 1990s, after Kim Jong Il was named heir apparent. Other possible contenders to replace Kim Il Sung, his sons by his second wife, Kim Pyong-Il and Kim Yong Il, were sent out of the country when they were old enough to attend school. Kim Pyong-Il later became an ambassador to a number of European countries, including Poland and Hungary, and Kim Yong Il would work in Germany, where he later died. Although having family members in prominent positions in a Communist government is not unusual, the family dynasty that has evolved in North Korea has never existed in any other Communist country before.

HEIR APPARENT

In February 1974, during an official meeting of the KWP's Central Committee, Kim Jong Il was appointed a member of the Political Bureau and oversaw the actions of the committee that would eventually assign Kim Jong Il as heir apparent to his father. From this point forward, no one referred to Kim Jong Il by his name, but rather by his honorific title, which was the Center of the Party. The following year at a similar meeting, Kim Jong Il was unanimously granted another title, that of Dear Commander, assuring his status to inherit his father's position as leader of North Korea. This was not yet official. That would come later, in 1980.

Around this same time, Kim Jong Il became involved in his father's concept of the Three Revolution Team Movement. The theory behind this movement was that in order to promote juche and to speed economic growth, management teams of KWP officials and other highly regarded people would travel around the

Kim Jong Il with his oldest son, Kim Jong Nam *(seated next to him)*. Kim Jong Il's sister-in-law, Sung Hye-rang, and her two children stand behind him.

country offering technical and scientific guidance to workers in factories, mines, and in the agricultural fields in order to improve their progress. In the process, these teams were to promote the theories of juche and to continue to rouse the masses in their allegiance to the Great Leader, Kim Il Sung.

Kim Jong Il spent much of the years between 1970 and 1980 working hard to strengthen the KWP, solidifying the principles of juche and sending out party members to pass the information along to the people. All the while, he also worked on his father's cult of personality, the personal myths of greatness that endeared people to their leader. It is believed that Kim Jong Il's efforts in this period to promote his father and his father's ideology might have been the crowning touch that would win his father's approval and Il Sung's recommendation of Kim Jong Il as his replacement.

DEATH OF THE GREAT LEADER

Although Kim Il Sung had enjoyed successes during his four decades of leadership, the last years of his dictatorship were not very prosperous. Kim Il Sung had cut off North Korea from foreign aid, reliant only on China, which by the 1980s was losing interest in supporting the country. The Soviet Union broke into separate countries in the 1990s, and each new nation struggled with its own economy and so could not provide much aid to North Korea. Despite the loss of money, Kim Il Sung insisted on creating an army of an estimated 1.2 million soldiers. The military budget ate away somewhere between one-fourth and one-third of the amount of money the country made.

As a result, a lot of North Koreans were living in extreme poverty. Countering this was the increased efforts by Kim Jong Il to make North

Koreans believe that his father was a god to whom they owed (and should give) everything. Kim Il Sung enjoyed meeting with his people; he attended to them, listening, speaking, and directing them as best he could. However, he also had a ruthless side. As he encountered or learned of someone talking against him, that person would either be publicly executed or would disappear, possibly imprisoned. People lived in awe and in fear of him.

Shortly, before Kim Il Sung died, former U.S. president Jimmy Carter made a trip to North Korea and met with Kim Il Sung in the mid-1990s. Through these efforts, the dictator promised to meet with U.S. officials one month later in Geneva, Switzerland, to talk about the possibilities of freezing his country's nuclear weapons development. Talks with leaders from South Korea also had been arranged for the end of the month. Both meetings would have been historical, but neither took place. At eighty-two years old, Kim Il Sung died of a heart attack in Pyongyang on July 8, 1994, the day of the scheduled talks in Geneva.

Thousands of North Koreans paraded through the streets after Kim Il Sung's death, openly mourning. One account, however, proclaims that if a person was caught not sufficiently mourning for Kim Il Sung, he or she would be put to death. There is a rumor that the crying turned into a type of contest to see who could cry the longest. There is also another account that claims that Kim Il Sung's heart attack might have come as the result of a heated argument with Kim Jong Il.

Although Kim Il Sung had named his son as heir to his regime, Kim Jong Il disappeared from view upon his father's death. He did not reemerge until three years later. Those three years had been declared a time of official mourning for Kim Il Sung, whose body was encased in a mausoleum, on public view, at the Kumsusan

Kim Jong Il oversaw the creation of this sixty-foot-tall (18.3 meters) bronze statue to honor his father, Kim Il Sung.

Memorial Palace. Kim Jong Il reportedly had the palace renovated for several hundred million dollars to make it into the world's largest mausoleum.

Kim Il Sung's birth and death dates are now national holidays. In respect for his father, Kim Jong Il retired, or abolished, the title of president and declared that his father would, for eternity, be the president of North Korea. In 1997, after the mourning period, Kim Jong Il then took the title of general secretary of the Korean Workers' Party and chairman of the National Defense Commission. One year later it was announced that going forward, these new titles would be the highest possible ranks in North Korea's government. Kim Jong Il was now North Korea's top leader.

CHAPTER FIVE

THE PRIVATE LIFE OF KIM JONG IL

Few verifiable facts about Kim Jong II, the world's most reclusive leader, are available about his public life. Even fewer facts are available about his private life. Through sources in Asia, such as people who have worked for Kim temporarily or North Koreans who have defected to other countries, a sketch of Kim's life can be drawn. The details, however, are sometimes contradictory. Still, they provide a glimpse into a life of a complex and often incomprehensible man. If Kim Jong II has done anything successful in his life, it is creating and maintaining the secrecy with which he runs his government.

AS A PLAYBOY

North Korea has been nicknamed the "Hermit Kingdom" due to its isolation. This nickname also reflects on the country's leader, who, unlike his father, is seldom seen in public, rarely travels outside of North Korea, seldom speaks in front of a crowd, and almost never smiles—in public at least. However, in reading accounts by people who have allegedly known Kim Jong Il, a different picture emerges of a man who likes to have fun and to have people around him.

Kim is often noticed for his short, five-foot-two (1.6 meters) stature, his pudgy shape, his puffed-up hairdo, the lifts in his shoes to make him appear taller, his large sunglasses that he often wears, and his usual khaki-colored jacket and trousers. "He's a mysterious person by design," Han S. Park told Carol Clark in a CNN interview. "Mystery is a source of leverage and power."

It has often been said that Kim loves to drink, eat, and woo women. He supposedly loves movies and has a collection of more than 10,000 videos, mostly from the United States, including the whole series of the television program *Desperate Housewives*, the *Godfather* movie series, James Bond movies, and Daffy Duck cartoons. It is also said that he owns many horses, all of them white. There is one story that claims Kim brought two gourmet pizza makers from Italy to create a

Kim Jong Il *(back center)* poses, in 1997, with members of the People's Army Youth Propaganda unit, which he once led.

kitchen from which they taught Kim's cooks how to make pizza.

Kim has been called generous. He has been known to give his highest officials, best friends, and loyal supporters fancy cars, like Mercedes. He is also generous to himself, apparently, as it has been said that he has several yachts and many Harley-Davidson motorcycles.

As a Husband, Father, and Family Man

Kim is said to have kept, at one time, a bevy of pretty, young Korean women around him all the time for his pleasure. There are many reports that he refers to these women, on occasion, as his doctors or his nurses. He is said to have fathered several children by several different women, not all of whom have been his wives.

By some accounts, Kim's first wife was Song Hae Rim, who lived with him for at least twenty years and gave him a son, Kim Jong Nam. It is possible that Kim never told his father about Song Hae Rim, who eventually left Kim, according to reports, because she could no longer stand Kim Jong Il's illicit affairs with other women. Others claim that she was Kim Jong Il's lover and mistress, but never his wife. Song Hae Rim died in Moscow, Russia, in 2002.

The distinction of first wife often goes to Kim Young Suk, a woman chosen for Kim by his father. Some believe that Kim Young Suk is still considered the dictator's official wife. There is no record as to what happened to her. Apparently, all records of her existence have been destroyed, although she may still be alive.

Kim Jong Il's second wife (or possibly just another lover) was claimed to be Ko Young Hee, the mother of another of Kim's sons, Kim Jong Chul. This son works in Kim Jong Il's old job at the KWP propaganda department. Ko Young Hee and Kim Jong Il also had a second child, Kim Jong Woong, who looks very much like his father. Although they might not have officially been married, Ko Young Hee played the role of first lady, an honor that his first wife never enjoyed. Ko Young Hee died while receiving treatment for cancer in Paris, France, in 2005.

There are rumors that Kim has numerous illegitimate children. A story circulating in 2006 claimed that Kim's secretary, Kim Ok, a woman who has been working for him since the 1980s, was introduced as his wife at a meeting with officials.

Kim Jong Il's eldest son, Kim Jong Nam, with his maternal grandmother in 1975.

Kim Jong Il's younger sister, Kim Kyung Hee, holds a powerful position in the North Korean government. Kim has used her as an example of the kind of loyalty he expects from everyone. It is reported that Kim Kyung Hee has been referred to as the first lady since the death of Ko Young Hee.

AS A LEADER

Before Kim assumed his father's reign, in the 1980s, rumors spread concerning several shocking incidents that are attributed to Kim Jong Il during this time. One involves the abduction of Japanese citizens, whom Kim reportedly wanted to use as spies. Another suggests that Kim was responsible for the 1983 bombing in Rangoon, Burma (now Myanmar), in which seventeen South Korean government officials were killed. Also, the downing of a South Korean airliner, which killed more than 100 people on November 29, 1987, is said to be the result of Kim Jong Il's orders. The reason the aircraft was downed, some officials speculate, may have been to discourage people from attending the 1988 Olympics held in South Korea. Defectors from North Korea have also claimed that, like his father, Kim Jong Il is known for executing or imprisoning anyone who does not agree with him.

Many people who have worked with Kim Jong Il or have visited him, such as former U.S. secretary of state Madeline Albright, have said that Kim Jong Il is intelligent and knows what he is doing. He has also been called daring, self-righteous, and cunning. Kongdan Oh, coauthor of *North Korea Through the Looking Glass*, said that Kim Jong Il "knows how to control his society and act strategically to shock . . . In that sense he's no different from a person like Stalin

Tearful Reunions

When Korea was divided into the North and South, many families were separated and prevented from leaving or entering North Korea. As part of South Korean president Kim Dae Jung's Sunshine Policy, a program was developed to reunite family members who have been separated by the thirty-eighth parallel. Between 2000 and 2006, fourteen rounds of reunions have taken place, bringing together relatives who had not seen each other for more than fifty years, since the Korean War.

Although the program was established as a step toward reunification of South and North Korea, problems have developed over the years. Only 100 people are allowed to meet at one time. It is also rumored that applicants in North Korea are given very strict guidelines concerning what they can and cannot say. Family members in South Korea often suffer from depression after meeting with their North Korean relatives, knowing that they may never see them again. The program was begun to foster peace between the two countries. However, after North Korea launched missiles in 2006, South Korea cut its aid program to the north, and Kim Jong Il stopped the reunion program shortly afterward.

or Saddam Hussein, and in many ways he's actually been more successful." Kim is also referred to as brutal, and there have been a lot of suspicions about his being responsible for many assassinations, even including members of his family, who have tried to defect.

Almost as soon as Kim took over the leadership of North Korea, the country's economy fell apart. This was not necessarily Kim's fault, but rather an accumulation of poor economic processes that his father held on to, as well as the circumstances of drought, floods, and diminishing interest on the part of China and Russia to supply North Korea with aid. By some reports, three million people died of starvation in the last half of the 1990s because the country could not raise enough food to feed its citizens, and life expectancy has dropped by five and a half years since the 1990s.

In order to increase his country's bank accounts, Kim reportedly engaged in criminal activities, such as dealing drugs. One story claimed that schoolchildren in North Korea were taught to harvest poppies, from which opium and heroin are processed. Besides opium, according to *Time* magazine in Asia, North Korea has been caught shipping out methamphetamines. North Korea sells these drugs to Japan, Russia, China, South Korea, and Taiwan. *Time* magazine estimated that one shipment discovered in Japan alone had a street value of $3 billion. The drug dealings have been going on for a long time, and since 1977, twenty North Korean officials, including diplomats, have been implicated in drug smuggling. Kim Jong Il also sells missiles to fellow rogue countries such as Iran and Pakistan. He is also known to make counterfeit U.S. money, the best in the world, one expert has claimed.

There are questions mounting about Kim's awareness of the world around him. Although Kim has access to the Internet and is said to keep abreast of several sources of foreign news, his firsthand experience in dealing with the outside world is extremely limited. He has traveled to China and Russia, but nowhere else. All the information that he receives about other countries is secondhand.

Kim Jong Il on his way to meet with Russian president Vladimir Putin in 2001.

There are reported signs of desperation inside Kim's world. With the economy failing, even the military is hurting from a lack of good nutrition as well as military supplies. There are reported shortages of gasoline and ammunition. Kim keeps a large group of the most loyal and well-trained bodyguards around him at all times. People who have met him confirm that he is very concerned for his life. This makes him uneasy among strangers. There were rumors of a failed assassination attempt in 2004, when the train Kim Jong II was traveling in passed through a North Korean station only hours before there was a huge explosion on the tracks. Kim's train carried several top officials of his regime on their way home from China, where they had discussed North Korea's nuclear program. Although the incident was claimed to be an accident, it caused a widespread stir in the international media as everyone questioned whether there were problems in Kim's regime.

CHAPTER SIX

KIM JONG IL AND INTERNATIONAL RELATIONS

As Kim Jong Il became more involved in his father's government, he took on the responsibility of explaining his father's juche ideology. He is said to have written more than 1,000 papers while in college explaining juche to his fellow students as well as to his professors. As minister of the Arts and Culture Bureau, Kim Jong Il would produce operas and movies promoting juche.

Kim Il Sung developed juche, and Kim Jong Il himself promoted it under his father's watch and further developed it in his own leadership. However, the three tenets—charip, chagu, and chawi—were never all fully realized. Charip (economic self-reliance) was difficult to implement, especially with the international threats of imposed sanctions on North Korea due to its nuclear ambitions. Chagu (political self-reliance), some pundits have suggested, would eventually falter because of the tremendous

From this 2005 photograph, the world gains a glimpse of the North Korean military, one of the world's largest armies.

pressure that the decrepit economy was placing on all aspects of the country. This left only chawi (military self-reliance) for Kim Jong Il to use to keep his country together under the ideology of juche.

FRAYING DIPLOMACY

In an attempt to increase his military power, Kim Jong Il pushed hard for the development of nuclear weapons. Toward this goal, in 1993, he announced that North Korea was quitting the Nuclear Nonproliferation Treaty, which was signed in 1970 by 187 countries to prevent the spread of nuclear arms. This signaled, or confirmed to those who were speculating, that Kim either was developing or possessed nuclear weapons.

To buffer this act, in 1994, North Korea and the United States signed an agreement, called the Agreed Framework, which stated that Kim Jong Il would freeze his nuclear weapons plan in order to receive aid in building two nuclear reactors. The reactors would be light water reactors, which Kim said his country needed to use as an energy source. The United States, in exchange, would assure no preemptive attacks on North Korea. This was not a treaty, according to the United Nations, but rather a signed memorandum. The Agreed Framework was brought about by Kim's withdrawal from the Nonproliferation Treaty and because the United States was building military forces around North Korea. The United States had been threatening to bomb North Korea's major nuclear reactor, which was capable of creating weapons grade plutonium. The agreement was made in hopes of stemming any further fears of aggressive military acts from both countries.

DEVELOPMENT OF MISSILES

Overt confrontations eased somewhat after the signing of the Agreed Framework, although the United States imposed sanctions on North Korea in 1996 and 1997 after Kim sold missile development information to other countries. After North Korea was caught selling missile technology to Pakistan, the country faced even more sanctions. But in August 1998, when Kim Jong II ordered a missile launch, which shot over Japan and into the Pacific Ocean, the United States and the rest of the world were caught by surprise. They had suspected the launch but were not prepared for the advanced technology that the missiles presented. Kim claimed that the launched missile had been used to put a satellite into space. World leaders were wary. What worried the international

Kim Dae Jung's Prize for Peace

In 2000, Kim Dae Jung, president of South Korea, won the Nobel Peace Prize for his attempts to bridge the political gap between North and South Korea. He was given this award for his Sunshine Policy, which advocates humanitarian efforts to ease the tension between North and South Korea. Kim Dae Jung was also praised for arranging a historical meeting between himself and Kim Jong II in June 2000 to mend the differences between the two nations. There was speculation that the Nobel committee might give a joint award to both the South Korean leader and Kim Jong II. However, Kim Jong II's reported crimes against humanity, including brutal beatings and political imprisonment of thousands of people, disallowed his award.

community was not the launching of a satellite. Producing plutonium was one thing, but if Kim Jong II had sophisticated missiles at his disposal, he could also deliver a nuclear weapon far from his own country.

In May 1999, William Perry, former secretary of defense under U.S. president Bill Clinton, met with North Korean officials asking for the elimination of North Korea's missile development. In exchange, the United States said it would lift all sanctions. Kim refused the offer, telling the United States that the lifting of all sanctions was already a part of the 1994 Agreed Framework. If the United States had not gone along with past agreements, why should Kim trust the United States? This lead to the countries becoming locked in a stalemate.

In 1999, George Tenet, then the director of the Central Intelligence Agency (CIA), told the U.S. Congress that according to intelligence reports, the CIA believed that North Korea was capable of delivering a bomb to Alaska and Hawaii, with a slighter possibility of Kim actually exploding a nuclear bomb somewhere in the continental United States. In May, President Clinton wrote a letter to Kim asking again for the North Korean leader to cease missile and nuclear development programs. The following year, the United States lifted some of its sanctions against North Korea, and Kim Jong II made a promise to freeze his weapons development.

KIM JONG IL AND THE REST OF THE WORLD

Although Kim Jong II promotes his father's concept of self-reliance, North Korea is very much dependent on aid from other countries. The North Korean economy is already failing, even with financial support from South Korea, China, and other countries. However, every time that Kim Jong II demonstrates his aggressive military programs, such as the testing of nuclear weapons, countries that once supported him tend to cancel their aid. On top of that, in order to control North Korea's missile and nuclear weapons programs, the United States, through the United Nations, promotes the use of sanctions against the country. The ones who suffer the most from these sanctions are the ordinary, working citizens who must endure extremely low wages and an extensive lack of everyday necessities such as soap and warm clothing. In addition, these people must live on a very poor diet, which consists mostly of meager amounts of grains. There are reports that many people are pushed to exist on eating grass and weeds.

Other nations are, therefore, caught between attempts to control the North Korean dictator through sanctions and the withdrawal of funds while trying to save the North Koreans from starvation.

KIM AND THE UNITED NATIONS

North Korea and the United Nations have come up against one another many times over the years. The usual situation is that the United Nations finds fault with North Korea, and North Korea then denies it. For example, the United Nations, through onsite inspections of North Korea's nuclear programs and sanctions, has tried to monitor Kim Jong II's aggressive military threats without much success. When North Korea tired of the invasion of UN influences in 2002, the United Nations' inspectors were expelled from North Korea. Then in 2006, after the United Nations voted to apply tougher sanctions against North Korea after it exploded a nuclear bomb, North Korea's UN ambassador, Pak Gil-yun, stated that the UN Security Council should congratulate North Korea's scientists for their accomplishments rather than seeking to punish North Korea.

Also the United Nations, in 2006, condemned North Korea for its human rights abuses, such as torture, public executions, forced labor, massive prison camps for political dissidents, and the absence of due process for prisoners. In addition, North Korea was charged for its programs of sexual exploitation of women and for setting up special camps to keep people with handicaps away from mainstream society. The deputy UN ambassador from North Korea, Kim Chang Guk, called the report biased.

KIM AND THE UNITED STATES

On September 27, 2000, dignitaries from North Korea and the United States signed a joint terrorism agreement. President Clinton took this as a positive sign that Kim might have wanted to mend fences between the two

U.S. president George W. Bush reacts harshly to North Korea's 2006 nuclear explosion.

countries. There was hope that the U.S. State Department would be able to remove North Korea from its terrorist list.

In October, Kim sent a top-ranking official to hand-deliver a letter from him to President Clinton. The future looked even a little brighter, as Clinton took this as a further sign that Kim was looking for peace. Kim, in return, received a statement from Clinton reinforcing the conditions of the 1994 Agreed Framework.

Plans were made for Madeline Albright, Clinton's secretary of state, to visit North Korea. One of Albright's goals during her October 24 visit was to set the stage for a historic meeting between Kim and Clinton.

In December 2000, the United States wrangled over a disputed presidential election between George W. Bush and Al Gore. Clinton had been advised that there could be a potential constitutional crisis in the United States. Because of this, Clinton was not able to visit Kim before the end of his presidency.

Kim, who looked at one point like he might be willing to negotiate with the United States, did a turnabout after Clinton's successor, Bush, in 2002 declared North Korea a part of the so-called Axis of Evil in the U.S. war against terrorism. From that point on, Kim persisted in developing nuclear weapons, despite U.S. sanctions against his country. Kim believed that North Korea could well be the next country that the United States would invade. President Bush, in the meantime, appealed to the United Nations to seek more sanctions against North

Korea. He has also refused to allow diplomatic negotiation with North Korea until Kim shows signs that he has ceased his program to develop nuclear weapons.

KIM AND SOUTH KOREA

If the United States was concerned about the possibilities of Kim Jong II dropping a nuclear bomb on its shores, the thought was more threatening to South Korea. This intensified the need, in some people's minds, for North Korea and South Korea to attempt a reunification. Unfortunately, it also increased the need for military reinforcements at the DMZ, where it was said that a million soldiers were stationed on each side, with powerful artillery aimed both north and south.

The idea of reunification between North Korea and South Korea has lingered between the two countries ever since the Korean War. The idea did not progress very far and actually deteriorated with the terrorist acts against South Korea in Burma and in the downing of the Korean airline, with both incidents allegedly carried out by Kim's agents. Tunnels under the DMZ were discovered in 1975, 1978, and 1990. These tunnels ran from North Korea to South Korea and were big enough for a whole army unit to pass through each hour. It was proved that they had been built from the northern border. Kim claimed that the tunnels were dug for coal-mining purposes. No evidence backed up this claim.

On the day of South Korea's newly elected Kim Dae Jung's inauguration, on February 25, 1998, he announced a new policy, which he referred to as the Sunshine Policy. It would be through this policy that Kim Dae Jung would promote peace between the two countries through reconciliation and cooperation. The three principles of the Sunshine Policy stipulated that South Korea would not make any armed provocation on the peninsula; South Korea would not attempt a takeover of North Korea; and it would actively push for reconciliation and cooperation with North Korea. The agreement suggested that although the reunification would take time, the process could start with simple trade agreements, the South's helping to ease the North's food shortages, and the North's easing up on visiting rights among family members who had been separated for more than fifty years.

The Sunshine Policy

The basis, or the story underlying, the name for the Sunshine Policy is found in one of Aesop's fables, "The Wind and the Sun." In this story, the wind and the sun compete to see who can make a man walking along a road take his coat off. The wind claims that he is stronger and that the contest is a simple one. The wind blows as hard as it can, but the man grabs his coat tighter around him, so the wind is unsuccessful. The sun, however, beams brighter and brighter upon the man, who begins to sweat and eventually takes off his coat. This story was on South Korean president Kim Dae Jung's mind when he came up with the name of South Korea's historic agreement with North Korea, the Sunshine Policy.

On June 15, 2000, a historic summit between North Korea and South Korea was held. An agreement was signed, stating that the two countries had decided to resolve the reunification question of the Korean peninsula. The issues mentioned in the Sunshine Policy appeared agreeable to Kim Jong Il, but he did not enter into any negotiations about missiles, nuclear weapons, or the deployment of troops away from the DMZ. President Kim Dae Jung won the 2000 Nobel Peace Prize for his efforts to reunite North Korea and South Korea. However, Kim Jong Il did not hold up his end of the bargain. He was supposed to reciprocate President Kim Dae Jung's efforts by personally visiting South Korea. He never did. In addition, by the end of Kim Dae Jung's presidency in 2003, South Korea's investment of more than $200 million in North Korea did not show any signs of improvement in their relationship. South Korean support of the Sunshine Policy began to dwindle.

In 2003, Roh Moo-Hyun was elected president of South Korea. Although it was during his term,

Kim Jong Il greets South Korean president Kim Dae Jung during their historic 2000 meeting.

in 2006, that North Korea tested a nuclear weapon, thus seriously injuring the diplomatic progress between South and North Korea, Roh has stated that he is not willing to give up on the Sunshine Policy between the two countries.

KIM AND CHINA

China, one of Kim Jong Il's strongest and most loyal supporters, appeared to be pulling in the reins after North Korea tested its nuclear bomb. Four major banks, according to *Newsweek* magazine, stopped making money transfers to long-standing North Korean accounts. China had also reduced shipments of food to North Korea, demonstrating a tougher attitude toward Kim than ever before. There was also speculation that the 11,000 barrels of oil (about 70 percent of North Korea's fuel supply) that China routinely sent to North Korea might also have been reduced significantly. In 2006, Kim had pulled out of the Six-Party Talks between China, the United States, Russia, Japan, North Korea, and South Korea intended to discuss nuclear weapons that begun in 2003. A few weeks after testing its nuclear weapon and talks between Kim Jong Il and Chinese officials, China made the announcement that Kim was willing to resume nonproliferation negotiations, though it has yet to happen.

KIM AND RUSSIA

Kim Jong Il's relationship with Russia had been an on-again, off-again affair. Kim's politics, for one, were more reminiscent of Stalin's version of socialism and Communism than the modernized Russian government was able to tolerate. However, Russia did support North Korea during the Korean War. Russia helped North Korea build its industry and may have helped it get started on its nuclear weapons program. However, the Soviet Union collapsed about the same time as the death of Kim Jong Il's father in 1994. After that, Russia no longer sent significant aid to North Korea.

After Kim tested a nuclear weapon, Russia was quick to point out that if any UN sanctions were to be placed on North Korea, they should not harm the country's people. Most of the

In 2006, South Koreans burn North Korean flags as they protest Kim Jong Il's aggressive military stance.

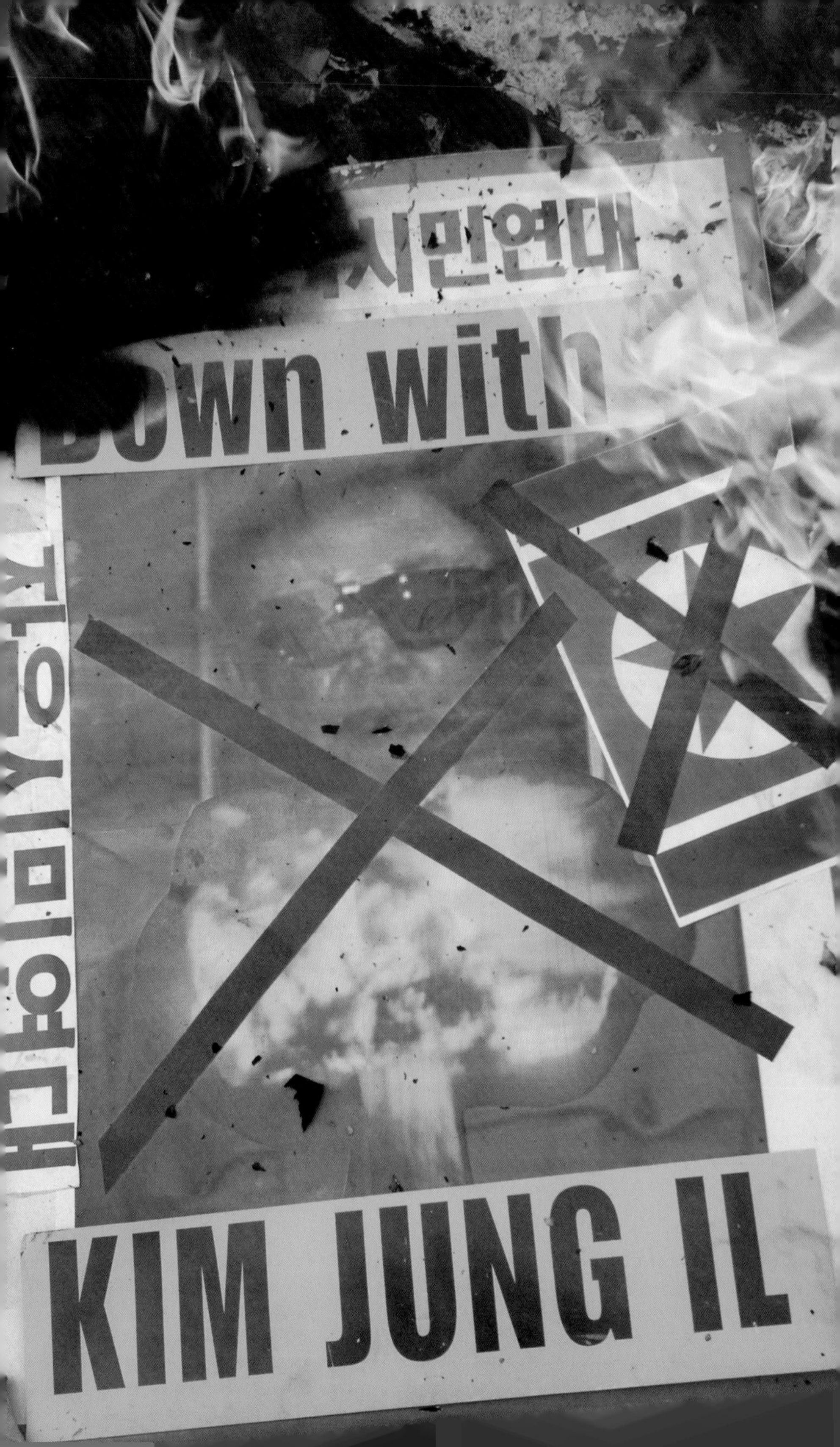
시민연대
Down with
KIM JUNG IL

emphasis, Russia advised, should be on getting North Korea back to negotiations. Russia and China share borders with North Korea. Neither country may support Kim Jong Il, but they do not want to see the United States take over the Korean peninsula with weapons pointed at their borders.

KIM AND JAPAN

North Korea and Japan have not established official relations since the defeat of Japan in World War II. Kim Jong Il made some attempts, but none was successful. Kim did meet with a Japanese official in 2002, the first-ever meeting between the two countries. Subsequent talks never materialized after Kim admitted that he was developing nuclear weapons and that North Korea was involved in the kidnapping of several Japanese citizens.

Despite this, Japan offered a large aid program to compensate for its takeover of the Korean peninsula in the early part of the twentieth century, said to be as large as $10 billion.

Japan was North Korea's third-largest trading partner, so Kim was interested in maintaining a relationship. However, in late 2006, Kim made an announcement that although his country would return to the Six-Party Talks, he was not welcoming Japan to join. Kim was disappointed that Japan did not support North Korea's desires to become a nuclear power.

KIM JONG IL'S POSSIBLE HEIRS

Kim Jong Il has fathered at least three sons and one daughter. The three men have all, at one point, been seen as possible heirs to his reign, thus continuing the Kim Dynasty.

Kim Jong Nam

Kim Jong Nam is Kim Jong Il's oldest son, born in 1971. His mother was Sun Hae Rim, probably not Kim Jong Il's wife but a longtime lover. Kim Jong Nam studied computer science abroad in Switzerland. For a while, he seemed a shoo-in for the distinction of heir apparent. He was given prominent positions in the Korean Workers'

Party, including the head of development of state computer programs. However, in 2001, he was arrested for using a false passport. Since then, he has been living outside of North Korea. Reporters have stated that upon spotting him, they have found him to be without bodyguards, a possible indication that he is no longer being considered as a future leader.

Kim Jong Chul

Kim Jong Chul is the son of Kim Jong Il and Ko Young Hee. He was born in 1981, studied in Switzerland, and works in the propaganda department of the Korean Workers' Party, as his father once did. In 2006, speculations of Kim Jong Chul being the heir apparent were very strong. However, because of his age, Kim Jong Chul might not be ready by the time his father wants to retire.

Kim Jong Woong

Kim Jong Woong was born in 1983 and is the youngest son of Kim Jong Il and Ko Young Hee.

Kim Jong Il, becoming more reclusive as he ages, makes a rare public appearance to inspect his troops in 2006.

Although he is also considered too young, reports have claimed that Kim Jong Woong might be Kim Jong Il's choice.

CONCLUSION

With reports of Kim Jong Il's health fading and his defiant testing of nuclear weapons, many of the world's most powerful leaders, despite their contradictory political beliefs, galvanized their thoughts about Kim. They did not know, as they have not known throughout his reign, if Kim was mentally strained or extremely cunning in his bizarre rejection of warnings from everyone not to develop nuclear weapons.

There is little understanding in the international community about what Kim Jong Il wants. Does he want power? Or does he want peace and prosperity? No one knows for sure what he might do in order to get what he wants. Is he willing to set off a nuclear bomb that could destroy the world? Or is he using the bomb only as a threat?

What is known is that his people are starving. Thousands of North Koreans are fleeing across the border to China to escape the hardships of Kim Jong Il's devastating rule. More are slipping into South Korea. What happens if throngs of people begin to leave North Korea? What will become of them? Who will take care of them? What effect will that have on those who are left behind?

Although the United Nations has placed sanctions against North Korea, no one knows for sure what impact they will have. Will the sanctions only anger Kim, thus forcing him into a corner, where all he has is the threat of nuclear holocaust? Or will the sanctions be the final blow that will make him surrender? Japan, South Korea, China, and Russia—North Korea's closest neighbors—are naturally concerned about forcing Kim Jong Il's hand. These countries stand to suffer the most. However, other countries, such as the United States, believe stricter sanctions are the only way to persuade Kim Jong Il to abandon his weapons program. With these unknowns, all the world can do is wait and watch him carefully and suspiciously because Kim Jong Il, among other things, is not only a dictator of a country with countless reports of human rights abuses, but also a terrifying leader who could potentially destroy the world with nuclear weapons.

TIMELINE

1904–1905 Japan and Russia go to war, fighting for control of the Korean peninsula in the Russo-Japanese War.

1910–1945 Japan annexes Korea and dominates its culture

1912 Kim Il Sung is born.

1919 Koreans stage massive protests against Japan's domination of their land.

1926 Kim Il Sung organizes the Down with Imperialism Union while living in exile in China.

1927 Kim Il Sung joins the Korean branch of the Communist Party.

1937–1945 The Second Sino-Japanese War between China (reinforced by Korea) and Japan when Japanese armies invade China through the Korean peninsula.

1941 Kim Il Sung marries Kim Jong-suk.

1941 Kim Jong Il is born.

TIMELINE

1946 Kim Il Sung University in Pyongyang is founded.

1948 Kim Il Sung becomes the first prime minister of North Korea.

1949 Kim Jong Il's mother, Kim Jong-suk, dies.

1950–1953 North Korea invades South Korea, leading to the Korean War.

1963 Kim Jong Il graduates from the Kim Il Sung University with a degree in political economy.

1973 Kim Jong Il is appointed chief of the Korean Workers' Party's Central Committees of Propaganda and Agitation Bureau.

1975 KWP Central Committee members assign the title of Dear Commander, signaling that Kim Jong Il is the heir apparent to his father's regime.

1980 Kim Il Sung announces that Kim Jong Il will succeed him as leader of North Korea.

1983 North Korea is accused of planting a bomb in Burma that kills seventeen members of a South Korean delegation, including four cabinet members.

1987 A Korea Air Lines jet explodes, killing all 115 aboard. The explosion is blamed on North Korea.

1994 Kim Il Sung dies on July 8. Kim Jong Il, his son, takes over leadership of North Korea.

2003 Six-Party Talks take place in Beijing between China, the United States, Russia, Japan, South Korea, and North Korea in hopes of averting a nuclear crisis.

2005 North Korea announces that it is dropping out of the Six-Party Talks and is building up its nuclear weapon arsenal.

2006 North Korea test-fires missiles and short-range rockets in July. In October, North Korea carries out its first underground nuclear weapons test. North Korea agrees to restart the Six-Party Talks.

Glossary

capitalism An economic system in which the production and distribution of wealth is mainly controlled by individuals or corporations, as opposed to businesses being controlled by the government. The economy is based on a free market system, which is competitive. This system is prevalent in the economic practices of the United States.

Communism A theory based on the principle of communal ownership of all businesses and property, often under the control of one political party that is in perpetual existence. In theory, under this economic system all people would work together and equally share in the bounty or profits.

Confucianism Based on the teachings of Confucius (551–479 BCE), a system of ethics that encourages love for humanity, respect of

one's parents, ancestor worship, and a strong
emphasis on education.

Demilitarized Zone (DMZ) An area set
aside that forbids any use of military weapons
or conflict. A demilitarized zone is usually set
up between two potentially warring groups of
people. The DMZ that separates North
Korea from South Korea is at the thirty-
eighth parallel.

imperialism The process of one empire (or
nation) extending its power over another
country, or of acquiring and holding colonies.

juche Official state policy of North Korea
created by Kim Il Sung that dictates that
North Korea base its political and economic
practices on self-reliance, with the three
main principles calling for independence in
politics, economy, and self-defense.

Korean War Lasting between 1950 and 1953,
a war between North Korea (supported by
China) and South Korea (supported by the
United States and United Nation) that ended
with the division of North Korea and South
Korea at the thirty-eighth parallel.

Maoism A form of Marxist-Leninist Communism formed by Mao Tse-tung, leader of China from 1949 to 1976, which includes principles of revolution and guerrilla warfare. The preferred term is Mao Tse-tung Thought.

Marxism An economic system developed in the mid-nineteenth century by Karl Marx, with assistance from Friedrich Engels, whose goal is to bring about a classless society and the end of the suppression of the masses caused by capitalism.

nuclear weapons Weapons that derive their destructive force from nuclear reactions that cause enough power to destroy entire cities. The United States was the first country to develop nuclear weapons, and it used them to end World War II. Other countries that are known to have nuclear weapons include the United Kingdom, France, Pakistan, India, China, Russia, and North Korea.

Russo-Japanese War War fought between Russia and Japan from 1904 to 1905 that ended in Japan's victory, giving Japan power over the Korean peninsula.

Sino-Japanese War There were two Sino-Japanese wars: one occurring between 1894 and 1895 between China and Japan, which concluded with a Japanese victory; and another between 1937 and 1945, which also ended in a Japanese victory and gave Japan control over Korea until the end of World War II.

Six-Party Talks Six nations (China, Russia, South Korea, North Korea, Japan, and the United States) agreed to meet in order to find a peaceful resolution to security concerns after North Korea retreated from the Nuclear Nonproliferation Treaty in 2003.

socialism Based on Marxism, the economic principle or step between capitalism and Communism in which workers jointly own production and benefit equally in the profits made. Everyone is of one class.

Stalinism The principles of Communism as defined and practiced by Joseph Stalin of the Union of Soviet Socialist Republics (USSR; formerly Russia), characterized by violent means of suppressing political dissidents, a

strong dictatorship, and aggressive international
policies.

Sunshine Policy South Korean policy toward
North Korea based on an old fable of a
competition between a cold wind and a strong
sun, with the warmth of the sun winning. The
policy stresses the importance of peaceful
cooperation and has reunification of the
Korean peninsula as its goal.

thirty-eighth parallel The line that separates
Communist North Korea from democratic
South Korea, arbitrarily drawn along the
thirty-eighth north line of latitude after
World War II in 1945.

For More Information

Human Rights Watch (HRW)
350 Fifth Avenue, 34th Floor
New York, NY 10118
(212) 290-4700
E-mail: hrwnyc@hrw.org
Web site: http://hrw.org/doc/?t=asia&c=nkorea

Korean Central News Agency (KCNA) of the
    Democratic Peoples Republic of Korea
    (North Korea)
E-mail: eng-info@kcna.co.jp
Web site: http://www.kcna.co.jp/index-e.htm

Life Funds for North Korean Refugees
A-101 Nishi Kata Hyteru
2-2-8 Nishi Kata, Bunkyo-ku
Tokyo, Japan 113-0024
Web site: http://www.northkoreanrefugees.com

Radio Free Asia (RFA)
2025 M Street NW, Suite 300
Washington, DC 20036
(202) 530-4900
E-mail: contact@rfa.org
Web site: http://www.rfa.org/english

WEB SITES

Due to the changing nature of Internet links, Rosen Publishing has developed an online list of Web sites related to the subject of this book. This site is updated regularly. Please use this link to access the list:

http://www.rosenlinks.com/nm/kijo

For Further Reading

Becker, Jasper. *Rogue Regime: Kim Jong Il and the Looming Threat of North Korea.* New York, NY: Oxford University Press, 2006.

Breen, Michael. *Kim Jong-Il: North Korea's Dear Leader.* New York, NY: John Wiley & Sons, 2004.

Dae-Sook, Suh. *Kim Il Sung: North Korean Leader.* New York, NY: Oxford University Press, 1995.

Ingram, Scott. *Kim Il Sung.* Farmington Hills, MI: Thomson Gale, 2004.

Jin, Tak, Kim Gang Il, and Pak Hong Je. *Great Leader, Kim Jong Il.* Tokyo, Japan: Sorinsha, 1985.

Martin, Bradley K. *Under the Loving Care of the Fatherly Leader, North Korea and the Kim Dynasty.* New York, NY: St. Martin's Press, 2004.

McCormack, Gavan. *Target North Korea.* New York, NY: Nation Books, 2004.

Oberdorfer, Don. *The Two Koreas.* New York, NY: Basic Books, 2002.

Oh, Kongdan, and Ralph C. Hassig. *North Korea Through the Looking Glass*. Washington, DC: Brookings Institution Press, 2000.

Palka, Eugene J., and Francis A. Galgano. *Geographic Perspectives: North Korea*. New York, NY: McGraw Hill, 2004.

Wit, Joel S., Daniel Poneman, and Robert L. Gallucci. *Going Critical: The First North Korean Nuclear Crisis*. Washington, DC: Brookings Institution Press, 2004.

Bibliography

Akaha, Tsuneo, ed. *The Future of North Korea*. London, England: Routledge, 2002.

Bae, Keun-min. *"Life Expectancy in North Korea Falls." Korea Times*. May 1, 2005. Retrieved December 7, 2006 (http://rangevoting.org/KoreaL.html).

Bong-uk, K. Chong, ed., North Korea: *Uneasy, Shaky Kim Jong-il Regime*. Seoul, South Korea: Naewoe Press, 1997.

Breen, Michael. *Kim Jong-Il: North Korea's Dear Leader*. Singapore: John Wiley & Sons (Asia) Pte Ltd., 2004.

Clark, Carol. *"Kim Jong Il: 'Dear Leader' or Demon."* CNN.com. Retrieved October 6, 2006 (http://www.cnn.com/SPECIALS/2000/korea/story/leader/kim.jong.il).

Economist. "Through the Looking Glass." July 8, 1999. Retrieved November 4, 2006 (http://

www.economist.com/research/backgrounders/
displaystory.cfm?story_id=220196).

Encyclopaedia Britannica Online. "*North Korea Under Kim Jong II.*" Retrieved December 7, 2006 (http://search.eb.com/eb/article-236884).

Gorenfeld, John. "*The Producer from Hell.*" *Guardian,* April 4, 2003. Retrieved November 2, 2006 (http://film.guardian.co.uk/print/ 0,,4640432-3181,00.html).

Guardian. "*Former Secretary Wins Heart of North Korean Leader,*" July 24, 2006. Retrieved October 6, 2006 (http://www.guardian.co.uk/ print/0,,329536506-1014490,00.html).

Ingram, Scott. *Kim II Sung.* Farmington Hills, MI: Blackbirch Press, 2004.

Jin, Tak, Kim Gang II, and Pak Hong Je. *Great Leader, Kim Jong II, Vol. 1 & 2.* Tokyo, Japan: Sorinsha, 1985.

Martin, Bradley K. *Under the Loving Care of the Fatherly Leader.* New York, NY: St. Martin's Press, 2004.

McClure, Laura. "*Understanding Kim Jong II,*" Salon.com. January 10, 2003. Retrieved

October 6, 2006 (http://dir.salon.com/story/
news/feature/2003/01/10/korea/index.html).

Oh, Katy, and Ralph Hassig. "*Kim Jong-il Through
the Looking Glass.*" Nautilus Institute. 2003.
Retrieved November 4, 2006 (http://nautilus.
org/DPRKBriefingBook/negotiating/Profileof
KimJong-il.html).

Palka, Eugene J., and Francis A. Galgano. *North
Korea, Geographic Perspectives.* New York, NY:
McGraw-Hill Companies, 2004.

Spaeth, Anthony. "*Kim's Rackets,*" *Time Asia.* June 2,
2003. Retrieved November 3, 2006 (http://
www.time.com/time/asia/magazine/printout/
0,13675,501030609-455850,00.html).

Index

ABOUT THE AUTHOR

Joyce Hart, a writer and published author, minored in Asian studies for her undergraduate degree. She studied the history, art, language, culture, and literature of some of the major Asian countries. She has published several nonfiction books for students, including those on social studies topics and contemporary literature. She lives in Washington State.

PHOTO CREDITS